Pedagogy and Space

PEDAGOGY AND SPACE

Design Inspirations for Early Childhood Classrooms

Linda M. Zane, EdD

Redleaf Press®
www.redleafpress.org
800-423-8309

Published by Redleaf Press
10 Yorkton Court
St. Paul, MN 55117
www.redleafpress.org

This book is based on *A Pattern Language: Towns, Buildings,
Construction* by Christopher Alexander, Sara Ishikawa, and
Murray Silverstein. Copyright © 1977 by Christopher Alexander.
Permission granted by the Center for Environmental Structure.

First edition 2015
Cover design by Jim Handrigan
Cover photograph by Linda M. Zane
Interior design by Erin Kirk New
Typeset in Chapparal, Glypha, and Tekton
Interior photos by Linda M. Zane
Printed in the United States of America
21 20 19 18 17 16 15 14   1 2 3 4 5 6 7 8

Library of Congress Cataloging-in-Publication Data

Zane, Linda.
   Pedagogy and space : design inspirations for early childhood
classrooms / Linda Zane.
      pages cm.

   Summary: "Colorful photographs of intentionally designed
spaces will inspire you as you dream, plan, build, and revamp
settings. Inspired by the groundbreaking architectural book A
Pattern Language: Towns, Buildings, Construction, this resource
aims to glean architectural information regarding important design
patterns in an environment and utilize them to provide insight
into early childhood environments that are both developmentally
appropriate and aesthetically pleasing"— Provided by publisher.

   Includes bibliographical references and index.
   ISBN 978-1-60554-358-1 (pbk.)
1. Education, Preschool—United States—Planning. 2. Child
care—United States—Planning. 3. Classroom environment—
United States.
I. Title.
   LB1140.23.Z36 2015
   372.21—dc23
                                        2014021504

Printed on acid-free paper

CONTENTS

Acknowledgments ix

Introduction | Why Classroom Design Matters 1

What Is the Feeling Conveyed by Different Classroom Environments? 2
How Does Your Own Classroom Stack Up? 3
Pedagogy and Space 3
Why I Wrote This Book 6

Part 1 | The Importance of Childhood Environments: What Does the Research Say? 9

Theory into Practice 9
The Importance of School Environments 14
A Systemic View of the Environment 15
Barriers to Change 17
Considerations for Change 18

Part 2 | Design Patterns for Early Childhood Classrooms 21

Category 1: Making Connections *(General Schemes of Connection)* 22
Mosaic of Cultures 23
Intimacy Gradient 25
Communal Eating 26
Classroom Workshop 29
Things from Your Life 30
Connection to the Earth 33

Category 2: Coming and Going *(Entrance and Exit)* 34
    Building Edge 35
    Entrance Transition 36
    Welcoming Reception 39
    Entrance Room 40

Category 3: On the Move! *(Circulation)* 42
    Flow through Rooms 43
    Short Passages 44

Category 4: Let the Sunshine In! *(Lighting and Color)* 46
    Indoor Sunlight 47
    Pools of Light 48
    Tapestry of Light and Dark 51
    Warm Colors 53

Category 5: A Place of My Own *(Room Structure)* 54
    Common Areas at the Heart 55
    A Space of One's Own 56
    Flexible Classroom Space 59
    Window Place 60
    Child Caves 63
    Bulk Storage 64

Category 6: Be Comfortable *(Seating)* 66
    Sequence of Sitting Spaces 67
    Different Chairs 68
    Stair Seats 71

Category 7: Take It Outside! *(Outdoor Spaces)* 72
    Adventure Playground 73
    Half-Hidden Garden 75
    Outdoor Classroom 76
    Opening to the Street 79
Applying What You've Learned 80

Part 3 | Design Patterns Tool Kits: Applying What You've Learned 81

Ready, Set, Go! 81
    Tool Kit #1: *Ready*: Reframe, Recruit, Record 81
    Tool Kit #2: *Set*: Story, Spark, Segment 83
    Tool Kit #3: *Go!*: Go What? Go How? Go When? Go Again 85
Pedagogy and Space within Your Classroom 87

Appendix: Design Patterns for Early Childhood Classrooms Worksheet 89
References 91
Index 95

ACKNOWLEDGMENTS

Many people have helped bring this book to fruition. A sincere thanks is extended to David Heath, Kyra Ostendorf, and those at Redleaf Press who have allowed me to share the concept of *Pedagogy and Space* with early childhood professionals everywhere. Thanks also to Danny Miller, whose editing contributions masterfully shaped the text into a polished final product.

A debt of gratitude goes out to the many Pittsburgh-based National Association for the Education of Young Children–accredited child care programs that graciously agreed to share their inspiring indoor and outdoor spaces. Photos from the following programs are shared within the pages of this book, and I am truly grateful to each for allowing me to capture elements of their wonderful programs. Many of those listed below have been dear friends for a long time, and some are new friends. Thank you to each for your fierce commitment to providing high-quality experiences to the children of Pittsburgh. Thank you as well to the Waldorf School of Philadelphia who generously contributed photos of their whimsical classroom spaces.

- The Campus School of Carlow University—Michelle Peduto, Executive Director
  http://campusschool.carlow.edu
- Carriage House Children's Center—Natalie A. Kaplan, President and Founder
  www.carriagehouse.org
- The Children's School at Carnegie Mellon University—Dr. Sharon M. Carver, Director and Professor
  www.psy.cmu.edu/cs
- Cyert Center for Early Education—Carla Freund, Administrative Director
  www.cmu.edu/cyert-center
- The Glen Montessori School—Jacqueline Downing Herrmann, Head of Education
  www.glenmontessori.org
- Noah's Ark Preschool—Gerda K. Moul, Director
  http://ourredeemer-peters.org/preschool.html
- Riverview Children's Center—Betty Liskowski, Director
  www.riverviewchildrenscenter.org
- Room to Grow Child Development Center—Carrie Dunkowski, Director
  www.ymcaofpittsburgh.org/room-to-grow

- Shady Lane School—Gina Capriotti, School Director
  www.shadylane.org
- Stepping Stones Children's Center— Lynn Kline, Director
  www.stepstonescc.org
- Tender Care Learning Centers (Robinson Township Site)—Charzzi White, Director
  www.earlyeducationpros.org/index.jsp
- The Waldorf School of Philadelphia
  http://phillywaldorf.com

I must express my love and gratitude to my ever-supportive husband, Paul, who is a constant source of strength, and whose patience and encouragement have seen me through many long days of writing. Much love and gratitude are extended to my daughters, Marissa and Rebecca, for their invaluable assistance at various stages during the development of the book. My parents, John and Betty Ann Manes, deserve a world of thanks for undergirding me since childhood with unconditional love and a sense of faith and purpose. And I am thankful to my God, who has led, is leading, and will lead me one step at a time, lovingly guiding me through whatever comes my way.

Pedagogy and Space

INTRODUCTION | Why Classroom Design Matters

Does classroom design matter to you? Does it impact the children in your care? How about the families who visit your program? You spend many of your waking hours in a particular classroom environment. How much time do you spend thinking about the design and arrangement of this environment?

For many of us, the design of our physical environment is as invisible as the air we breathe or the sun that shines—we just don't think about it. These invisible elements tend to draw our attention only when they are missing or obviously deficient. But make no mistake, the physical environment in which you spend your time, whether you consciously realize it or not, matters a great deal.

If a picture is worth a thousand words, photographs of classroom environments should speak volumes about the learning experiences that occur there. Look closely at the following photographs of early childhood classroom environments. Each environment has similar elements, but many differences can be seen. If you were a child or teacher in any of these classrooms, how do you think your daily experiences might differ?

What Is the Feeling Conveyed by Different Classroom Environments?

Consider the lighting. What is the source of light in each classroom? Do the classrooms seem light and airy, utilizing lots of natural light? Or are they dark and claustrophobic, using mostly artificial light?

Consider the materials used in the classroom decor. Are these materials natural or artificial? Do they seem current and fresh, or do they hearken back to an earlier era? Do they project a sense of warmth or a feeling of institutionalization?

Consider the arrangement of furniture within the classroom. Is the room spacious, allowing for children and teachers to circulate between areas? Or does the room seem crowded, leaving little room to maneuver and visit friends?

Consider the learning opportunities afforded by each classroom setting. Does the focal point of the room appear to be play oriented, or is it academically driven? Are interesting, engaging activities visible—ones that will promote creative, divergent thinking? Does the atmosphere send a message of child-centered exploration, or does it seem to reflect teacher-centered instruction?

How Does Your Own Classroom Stack Up?

Now consider your own classroom or program. How does it compare with those shown here? If you entered your classroom as an outsider, what messages might you pick up based on the physical environment?

The purpose of this book is to convince you that classroom design does indeed matter. It matters a great deal. Classroom environments matter to the children who spend many hours in them; they matter to the teachers who plan, teach, and live in them; and they matter to families and visitors who pass through on a daily basis.

Pedagogy and Space

As educators, *pedagogy*—the art and science of teaching—lies at the heart of our profession. We study the most current teaching techniques and search for ways of scaffolding a child's learning toward continuously higher levels. We provide learning opportunities that are hands on, minds on, and feelings on, always striving to engage each child's interest and attention. We know that children build beliefs and knowledge through active engagement with the world around them, and that they make sense of new information within the context of previous experience.

Classroom design can have a tremendous impact on your effectiveness as an early childhood educator. The physical environment of the entirety of your school, as well as your individual classroom, can support successful pedagogy in the following ways:

■ *Reinforce and Complement Your Teaching Philosophy*

Any visitor to your program should take one look at your classroom environment and instantly discern your teaching beliefs and philosophy.

Are you a constructivist educator? Do you believe in the power of play? Then your classroom should contain complex, open-ended learning centers where the focal point is child-centered play.

Are you a Montessori educator? Do you believe in the importance of child-oriented works? Then your classroom should reflect a carefully prepared environment with Montessori materials and curriculum areas throughout.

Are you an anthroposophical educator, following the practices of the Waldorf approach? Then your classroom should be full of natural materials, and your classroom walls should be painted in a pale, translucent color.

The classroom design, materials, arrangement, and colors should speak to all who enter, communicating the foundational beliefs on which your program has been built. If this is not currently the case within your school, this should be an area of focused attention for you and your colleagues.

■ *Support Developmentally Appropriate Practices*

As early childhood educators, our mission is one of fostering a child's growth and development through developmentally appropriate practices. Children in our programs should be supported through play materials and activities that are appropriate for their stage of development. The physical environment of the classroom is of critical importance in this effort.

There are many things to consider when evaluating the developmental appropriateness of a classroom space. Are the play materials safe, and do they foster scaffolding to higher levels of understanding? Are the children regularly exposed to a variety of open-ended materials that heighten their levels of problem solving, inquiry, and creativity? Does the room arrangement and the placement of learning centers promote a young child's need for small, comfortable spaces that promote collaboration with peers? Are different, yet complementary, play items within close proximity in order to facilitate the blending of materials between learning center areas? Are the play materials sufficiently complex, allowing for appropriate levels of challenge, yet not exceedingly complex, leading to frustration? As you consider the implications of pedagogy and space within your program, reinforcing developmentally appropriate practices is a critically important factor.

■ *Promote a Variety of Learning Styles*

All children absorb environmental stimuli and make sense of new information through their senses. Your classroom should help children learn and grow by promoting the use of their senses—auditory, visual, and kinesthetic/manipulative. The number of materials throughout the classroom that utilize each learning style should be of equal abundance; the room arrangement should invite the children to partake in sensory activities without fear of noise or distraction.

■ *Aid in Behavior Management*

Space can be an invaluable pedagogical tool as you manage and guide children toward making appropriate behavioral choices. Strategically placed learning areas that allow for uninterrupted play can drastically eliminate problem behaviors. A child who is actively engaged in playful activities, using her mind and body expressively and experientially, will have little need to make poor behavioral choices.

In contrast, children who are bored and left with little to appropriately engage their minds or bodies will be much more likely to look for creative ways of entertaining themselves— typically in ways that are more rambunctious or rowdy. Likewise, large open areas of space that do not contain learning centers can often invite aimless running around and disengaged children. Boredom rarely leads to positive behavioral choices. Classroom space and materials can play an important role in maintaining positively engaged hands and minds.

■ *Be Aesthetically Pleasing*

A clean, pleasant, and aesthetically pleasing environment can greatly enhance the space that you inhabit every day. Each teacher, child, family member, and visitor deserves to spend his or her time in a space that is both pleasant and inspiring. Such an environment sends a message of respect and appreciation for all who inhabit the space.

Furthermore, the more aesthetically pleasing the environment, the more we are subliminally encouraged to maintain the space at its current high level. Sustaining cleanliness and beauty by both educators and children is much easier once a high standard has been set for all.

Why I Wrote This Book

As the former director of a National Association for the Education of Young Children–accredited early childhood program, I must confess that classroom design used to be rather low on my list of priorities. My role as the leader of the program was to ensure that the children and families received the best possible care. Shepherding a developmentally appropriate teaching staff;

creating relationships with teachers, children, and families; and caring for the health and welfare of everyone involved seemed of utmost importance. Little time was left for seemingly frivolous concerns such as classroom design.

With age comes wisdom, and I can now see that I was unknowingly overlooking a critical piece of the puzzle—the intersection of pedagogy and space. I have since witnessed a variety of early childhood spaces—some that are dull and lifeless, and others that exude the vibrancy and excitement that only come from

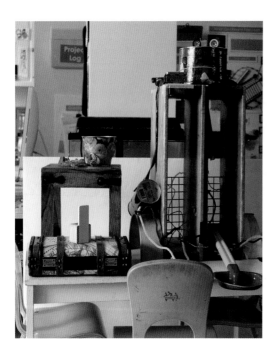

paying attention to the classroom environment. If only I knew then what I know now . . . Well, suffice it to say that my early childhood program would have looked very different.

Granted, the classrooms in my child care center weren't horrible, and there were quite a few elements of which I am still proud, including turning a stairwell landing into a "bear cave," a small space that was home to a huge stuffed bear where a teacher could read with her group of children. But the majority of the program was merely functional, without any attention paid to the "extras"—creative lighting solutions, inviting window places, and the use of natural materials, to name a few.

This book has grown out of my personal need for an expanded understanding beyond the insular field of early childhood education. Architecture was always instinctively intriguing to me, and my physical space has always impacted my mood. But having a daughter who was studying to be an architect brought those instincts to the forefront of my attention. Once I was in the mind-set to understand, blending architectural insights with early childhood expertise seemed quite natural and

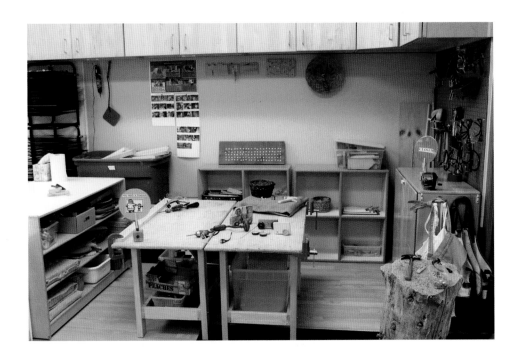

logical. Age and wisdom have brought me out of the fog.

Of course exciting spaces lead to more engaging exploration and critical thinking opportunities! It's obvious to me now that unique lighting can provide warmth and interest to a room. And using a variety of types of chairs naturally adds interest, comfort, and expanded relationship opportunities. So many ideas all within reach— if only I had discovered them earlier!

Hence this book. It is not too late for you to transform your space into a truly unique environment. I hope the patterns and suggestions found in this text will encourage you to take an unbiased, objective look at your classroom. Many simple changes can be made to transform your room into a great space that engages the hearts and minds of those who spend time within.

PART 1

The Importance of Childhood Environments: What Does the Research Say?

Theory into Practice

When considering the foundational educational approaches that one associates with early childhood education, it's easy to see the considerable role that *environment* plays within the practice of each approach. The physical characteristics of any classroom are an outward manifestation of its philosophy; consequently, the behaviors and educational programs are equally impacted (Horne Martin 2002). Conversely, if one's philosophical approach to education is vague and undefined, the physical environment will lack focus and purpose. The teacher's philosophical beliefs about teaching and learning should be reflected in her pedagogical methods, supported by the materials and arrangement of the classroom space. A harmony should exist between space and learning; form should follow function by adapting the classroom space to harmoniously support the approach to learning found within (Montgomery 2008). The importance of childhood environments, as reflected by

the practices of the constructivist educational approach, the Reggio Emilia approach, the Waldorf approach, and the Montessori approach, are explored below.

■ *Constructivist Educational Approach*

The theory of constructivism, which strives to explain how a child builds his understanding of the world, is fundamentally based on the importance of environment. A child's construction of knowledge does not result from concrete bits of information that are memorized; rather, knowledge construction is a dynamic experience that is continuously built through interactions with the world (Ackermann 2004). Children use their prior knowledge of the world, along with current experiences within the spaces they inhabit, to gain a greater understanding of life. Each new experience allows the child to build, modify, and reinterpret perceptions; children constantly alter their conceptual understandings, aided by environmental interactions

Learning centers play an important role in constructivist early learning programs. Exposure to a variety of materials, typically arranged by content area, helps children in their physical, intellectual, emotional, and social growth.

(Grabinger and Dunlap 1995). A child's lived environment therefore plays a decisive role in the quality and depth of his knowledge attainment—both in and out of school. For this reason alone, the spaces in which children live and learn serve an elemental role in their growth and development.

■ *Reggio Emilia Educational Approach*

The Reggio Emilia approach elevates the importance of the environment by identifying it as a child's "third teacher," along with the child's parent and the classroom teacher (Halpin 2007;

Strong-Wilson and Ellis 2007). The Reggio Emilia approach believes that classroom spaces have an equal voice to parents and teachers. By way of invitation, the spaces and materials can speak to the children, offering aesthetically interesting and creatively challenging exploration. Through documentation, long-term projects are captured for posterity along with written and photographic evidence of the spaces involved. The documentation in a Reggio Emilia classroom reflects the history of the relationships between people, space, and pedagogy, creating wonderful representations of children's learning and development.

Evidence of artfully designed spaces abounds within a Reggio Emilia–inspired program. The documentation of children's projects, attention to light, and presence of bright, cozy spaces that are aesthetically inspiring are hallmarks of the importance placed on the environment within a Reggio Emilia–inspired early learning program.

■ *Waldorf Educational Approach*

Rudolf Steiner's beliefs about education and life are reflected within Waldorf schools (as they are called in the United States; in Europe they are typically referred to as Steiner schools). Steiner's holistic approach of incorporating the body, mind, and spirit is infused in all aspects of the physical classroom space. Steiner was relatively prescriptive regarding the ideal classroom space, which was an outgrowth of his spiritual ideas and his concern for establishing a proper foundation for children. All Waldorf classrooms exhibit a distinctive aesthetic environment, as reflected in the wall colors and painting treatments, natural materials, artwork, draped fabric, and unfinished wooden imaginative toys (Uhrmacher 2004). Steiner believed that light, color, and form were all crucial ways to support a child's spirit—all equally critical aspects of a Waldorf school's distinctive physical environment.

Learning spaces that promote fantasy, imagination, and creativity are typically found within a Waldorf school. The use of natural, unfinished play materials, along with fanciful draping and room coloration all point to a learning environment that upholds Rudolf Steiner's belief in nurturing the whole child.

■ *Montessori Educational Approach*

Maria Montessori's beliefs regarding the ways children learn best are mirrored within the Montessori educational environment. Montessori believed that children grow within six-year cycles of development, each characterized by certain sensitivities that must be recognized and enhanced by both adults and the physical environment. Every Montessori classroom exhibits a "prepared environment" containing "self-correcting materials," which allow the child to independently interact with the materials and then self-check for accuracy, all housed within a number of curriculum areas (Edwards 2002, 9). Montessori spaces should reflect beauty and order, allowing the child to have long spans of time during which she is immersed in real work. To stress the importance of a child's development through engaging in meaningful work, classroom materials within the Montessori

Maria Montessori's belief that a child will respond positively to a carefully prepared environment, filled with self-correcting materials arranged in left-to-right progression on orderly shelves, is evidenced within any Montessori classroom. The works are arranged within curriculum areas, allowing for freedom within limits and a child's growing ability to practice self-discipline.

approach are called "works." Every aspect of the Montessori philosophy is both supported by and demonstrated through the physical environment, encouraging a student's freedom within limits and focused self-discipline. Similar to the Reggio Emilia and the Waldorf educational approaches, the Montessori classroom clearly and distinctly echoes its philosophical beliefs—the outward manifestation of the pedagogy of space.

The Importance of School Environments

Because the environment plays such a fundamental role within the development of a child, it stands to reason that much attention would be devoted to the architectural spaces occupied by children. Although each of the educational approaches mentioned above (constructivist, Reggio Emilia, Waldorf, and Montessori) has a distinct aesthetic resulting from its philosophical beliefs, the majority of schools do not reflect this precedent. In his article titled "Utopian Spaces of 'Robust Hope': The Architecture and Nature of Progressive Learning Environments," author David Halpin (2007, 247) claims that "architecture for childhood" has not been as serious a consideration as it warrants. According to Halpin, any attention paid to architecture for children has unfortunately been dominated by adult concerns, including economic and professional considerations. While there is no broadly accepted utopian architectural theory dictating the most appropriate educational environments for children, nearly all educators would agree that the spaces children inhabit are of critical importance.

A number of researchers and experts have investigated the impact of school environments on children's growth and development. Researchers have also addressed the importance of school environments in regard to teachers, families, and the community. According to Leanne G. Rivlin and Carol S. Weinstein (1984), schools are places where learning, socialization, and psychological development coincide. Because children spend many of their waking hours there, schools must be recognized as crucial places that maintain a significant and continuing presence in children's lives.

Children certainly do spend a great deal of their time in schools. The U.S. Environmental Protection Agency (EPA, accessed 2014) reported that the average American schoolchild spends approximately 1,300 hours in a school building each year. And a growing number of those schools are aging and/or dilapidated. Currently, the average age of a public school building in the United States is forty-two years, and more than 75 percent of U.S. public schools were built before 1970. According to the most recent comprehensive federal report on the condition of American public schools, at least

$127 billion would be needed to bring all of the nation's schools into good condition (U.S. Department of Education 2000).

If a growing number of American schools are aging and/or dilapidated, what message does that send regarding the importance of a child's education? The way in which a school building is designed and maintained sends a clear message to the children, staff, and community about the value placed on the activities occurring within (Uline, Tschannen-Moran, and DeVere Wolsey 2009). Students subjected to school buildings with chipped and peeling paint, leaking roofs, and boarded windows could naturally conclude that education is not valued by their community—and the unfortunate addendum to that message is that *they* are not valued. Many students are resilient and do not allow such barriers to stand in the way of their education, but such subliminal messages can only lead to long-term harm within a community. Conversely, time spent on making practical and artful changes to a school's environment increases the complexity of meaning and purpose that teachers and students assign to their educational experiences.

A Systemic View of the Environment

A classroom is more than a collection of items found within a space; it is a complex system of relationships. One finds an intricate inter-relationship between the physical structure of the room, the arrangement and distribution of space, and the individuals (teachers and students) who share the space. When time is spent improving the physical environment, the classroom system and its relationships are likewise significantly improved (Horne Martin 2002). For true integrity to be present within the space, the classroom environment should be a direct reflection of the educators' philosophical approach.

The school must also be viewed as a series of interconnected systems of communications and relationships (Rinaldi 1998). These relationship-oriented systems must include all stakeholders, including teachers, children, and parents. Such a systems focus will naturally extend to the spaces within the school. The architecture should support both the pedagogy and the relational systems that are undertaken at the school (Rinaldi 1998). Ideally, classrooms should open to shared spaces where relationships among groups of children and adults can be fostered throughout the day.

Classroom physical environments should also be systems that support emotional growth and well-being. Space can be structured to reflect a welcoming and caring tone to all who enter. Children who are intellectually and emotionally engaged are more likely to express feelings of support and security. As discovered by one research study, when asked to describe favorite (important, liked, and valued) places in their daily surroundings, both children and adolescents chose places that were relaxed, calm, and comfortable (Korpela 2002). This finding indicates that favorite places are essential for providing an emotional release and imparting a restorative experience—desired emotional responses that help to promote learning.

■ *The Classroom Environment and Achievement*

A school building that provides a high-quality learning environment is essential for student success. Research has linked student achievement with optimal physical environmental characteristics. Several studies have shown, on average, a five- to seventeen-point increase on achievement tests for students who attended a more modern, above-standard school building rather than an antiquated, more substandard building, regardless of the socioeconomic status of the school district (Berner 1993, Cash 1993, and Hines 1996). It is also important to note that, as a group, these studies reflected a variety of student populations—Washington, DC, rural and urban Virginia, and North Dakota. Together they present a unified rationale for the impact of a school's physical environment on student achievement.

Building age has also been correlated with student achievement. The age of a building is not important per se, but most newer buildings tend to have better heating, air-conditioning, and ventilation, as well as improved acoustics—all of which lead to classroom environments that are more conducive to learning (Earthman and Lemasters 1996). Many older buildings may not have sufficient or appropriate lighting. Because of the advances in building materials that support a more positive learning environment, students in more modern buildings have been shown to outperform students in older buildings on achievement tests (Earthman 2002).

The school's physical environment has also been shown to influence student attendance and dropout rates. In a 2004 study, using data from 226 Houston Independent School District schools, David Branham (2004) discovered that schools that were in poor structural shape—those using temporary rather than permanent structures, and schools without adequate custodial upkeep—were associated with higher dropout and lower attendance rates. Branham concluded that the negative physical environment and lack of attention to school facilities led to performance inadequacies.

Color used within the classroom can be indirectly related to student performance as well. Kristi S. Gaines and Zane D. Curry (2011) performed a thorough review of the prevailing research literature, investigating the effects of color on learning and behavior. Their analysis led them to conclude that the most effective color schemes for the foundation of a room are warm neutral colors, such as tan or sand. Additionally, the wall that students see after looking up from working at their desks should be a medium tone within the same color range. Contrary to the preferences of many teachers, the researchers found that strong or primary colors are not effective, and softer colors, such as pastel greens or blues, are preferred. Also, using different colored tape to indicate boundaries within the room can benefit all students, as well as incorporate children's individual color preferences in a variety of ways. Gaines and Curry concluded that color can impact student attention, behavior, and achievement, and it should be an important consideration within classroom design.

Barriers to Change

Quite often one barrier to making changes in a classroom environment stems from a human tendency to see things only as they are right now, rather than how they could change and improve—especially when a teacher sees many daunting limitations within the classroom space. A number of research studies have found that a classroom's current arrangement of physical space has a great deal to do with maintaining the status quo, rather than searching for ways

to incorporate more effective teaching practices (Woolner et al. 2012). For instance, Sandra Horne Martin (2002) found that the more traditional configuration of placing desks in rows within secondary school classrooms was associated with traditional teacher-directed teaching methods. This contrasts with more student-centered modes of teaching where students work at tables in collaborative groups or perform independent tasks within a variety of unique seating spaces in and out of the classroom.

Established cultural norms promote the notion of a classroom having a privileged front space. In our mind's eye, many of us carry traditional scenes of teachers lecturing in front of the class; this historic classroom schema can serve as a barrier to environmental change. Such a classroom setup can also prove to be less effective for all learners. Many who teach in the classic classroom setting can attest that often students who choose to minimize academic challenge and personal exposure gravitate toward the seats that are farthest from the front, usually around the perimeter of the classroom (Montgomery 2008). From the moment the students walk through the doorway, they quickly evaluate the room arrangement; if the room contains rows of desks, they sit where they feel most comfortable and where they will be either visible or invisible. If the room is filled with collaborative tables or interesting seating areas that are scattered about the room, students react accordingly. Therefore, one can conclude that students are guided toward learning expectations based on the space, since the room arrangement signals the activities expected. The form and nature of the setting impact students' anticipated experiences, just as they subtly lead the instructor toward preconceived notions of the types of learning that should occur, as well as his or her role as purveyor of knowledge.

Similarly, David R. McNamara and David G. Waugh (1993) deduced that teachers appeared to group children for collaborative work as dictated by the available furniture already in the room. Placing students in working groups of four to six students was typical. McNamara and Waugh concluded this was not a pedagogical decision, aimed at improving group cohesion, but rather a practical one, prescribed by table size and configuration. It often appears that the existing physical arrangement lends itself to maintaining the current state of affairs rather than seeking out substantive changes.

A barrier to change could also result from a lack of environmental or design training within teacher preparation programs. Jeffrey A. Lackney and Paul J. Jacobs (2002) discovered that, among the twelve national board certified teachers they interviewed and observed, none reported having any preservice training on design principles. Likewise, none of the

educators reported receiving any instruction on adapting their physical classroom setting to be more complementary to the curriculum. Lackney and Jacobs discovered that this lack of environmental knowledge led to the teachers relying solely on trial and error rather than sound research-based design principles.

Teacher preparation programs that ignore topics related to the classroom physical environment send an unfortunate message that such matters are trivial and unimportant. By offering such insights, a teacher education program could be deepened and strengthened. Lackney and Jacobs also recommend that teacher preparation programs offer hands-on experience with classroom physical environments. Preservice educators should be allowed to manipulate the physical environments of classrooms within a variety of age levels, testing their design ideas and adapting classroom space to better accommodate curricular decisions.

Considerations for Change

Education in the twenty-first century must change in order to adapt to an increasingly global view of the world, aided by a tidal wave of new technologies. Technology is "wiring" children's brains differently than previous generations, leading to differing educational abilities and requirements—starting with the youngest toddlers who adeptly navigate a tablet device or smartphone. We are caring for infants and toddlers who will be designing and manufacturing technological devices that do not even exist today. Faced with an ever-changing world that requires adaptability to the knowledge and skills necessary for success, one must consider ways in which children's classroom spaces reflect the dynamic needs occurring within education (Pearlman 2010). There is an increasing call for schools to transition from places filled with teacher-directed, whole-group instruction, to spaces reflecting learner-centered, collaborative, and project-based learning, aided by available technological tools. Schools of the future must incorporate a variety of learning zones, allowing for collaboration among peers and interactive projects that incorporate an integrated curricular focus (AAF and KnowledgeWorks Foundation 2005). Children of today are not the same as children of yesterday: their learning tools, modes of thinking, and skill needs are continuously changing. Their classrooms and learning spaces must likewise mirror the twenty-first-century revolution.

One important trend in school design centers on the inclusion of multiple voices during the investigatory and planning stages. Collaborative school design can lead to long-term, successful, and sustainable spaces for children (Woolner et al. 2012). In an *Improving Schools* journal article

titled "Changed Learning through Changed Space: When Can a Participatory Approach to the Learning Environment Challenge Preconceptions and Alter Practice?", the authors posit that involving all stakeholders—children, parents, teachers, school administrators, and community members—is a necessary part of any design process. Architects and builders are often unfamiliar with the needs of a particular school. Consulting with school administrators is typically part of the planning process; however, this leads to a narrowing of appreciation and understanding of all that can be accomplished by including additional perspectives and points of view. The consultation of those directly involved in the daily running of the school can lead to greater levels of long-term satisfaction, as well as the improved use of the space. Participatory design, especially among educators and other staff members, increases buy-in and appreciation of the new surroundings, leading to greater use of the space. As is often the case, the greater one's level of involvement is from the beginning, the more intense one's interest, desire, and use will be at the end.

Researchers within the fields of early childhood education and the sociology of childhood have shown an increasing level of interest regarding the importance of allowing the voices of young children to be heard within the planning process. Alison Clark and Peter Moss developed the Mosaic approach (Clark 2010; Clark and Moss 2001, 2005) as an extension of their desire to be respectful of children's ideas and allow them to engage in meaningful discussions about their surroundings. The Mosaic approach consists of two stages. The first stage involves children and adults gathering documentation relevant to the task. Pieces of the Mosaic that are used for documentation include child observations, child conferencing (similar to focus group discussions), cameras (photography by the child), tours (child-led tours of the school and grounds), mapping (as a result of the tour), and role playing (using toy figures) (Clark and Moss 2001). The second stage involves the whole of the data being brought together, allowing for dialogue, reflection, and interpretation. After the pieces of the Mosaic documentation are gathered, they are discussed and thoughtfully processed among all of the stakeholders—teachers, children, and parents—with any number of combinations participating at any one time. Such reflections and interpretations allow for themes and patterns to emerge, revealing the children's views on their interior and exterior environment. The Mosaic approach allows children to be active, competent participants and skilled communicators, rather than passive and voiceless partakers of that which is given by adults.

Children and young people are increasingly being recognized as competent members of society, active in shaping public structures and social identities (Burke and Grosvenor 2003). For too long, authentic invitations to participate in the complex challenges of school change have not been open to young people. Schools are often places of adult-imposed control—control in the buildings inhabited, the space created, and the materials provided. Control is imposed within the cultural conventions and institutional practices of school, such as being segregated by age, following a structured timetable of events, and executing rule-driven activities. A twenty-first-century mind-set requires a shift in perspective, encouraging an openness and transparency within the learning environment, and sparking the passion of the learner as he is involved in the nature, use, and design of the school. Certainly, any educator believing in a true pedagogy of space should welcome the opinions and desires of children; it is they who are ultimately the active partakers of the benefits (as well as the detriments) of that space. As you proceed with your own evaluation of your physical spaces, I urge you to consider the unique ideas and perspectives of all of the stakeholders—including the children—and honestly invite each to partake in the process of school change.

PART 2

Design Patterns for Early Childhood Classrooms

Published in 1977, *A Pattern Language: Towns, Buildings, Construction* (Alexander, Ishikawa, and Silverstein 1977) sought to present a new common language to the field of architecture based on years of practical knowledge gained from planning and building. Christopher Alexander's "patterns" represented an attempt to present a solution-oriented language to describe architectural configurations, an approach that has proven useful for many within the field of architecture and design (Nair, Fielding, and Lackney 2009). This approach should also prove to be useful for those in the field of early childhood education.

Each design pattern listed here was inspired by patterns found within Christopher Alexander's seminal work. Alexander stressed that architectural patterns are intended to support human relationships and to foster connectivity between all those who cross paths within any space. Many of the architectural patterns promoted by Alexander perfectly complement an early childhood classroom setting and provide solutions that will enhance both an educator's and a child's experience within the space.

For our purposes, we have grouped the patterns into seven categories. Within each category, you will find several of Alexander's specific patterns. The number in parentheses refers to Alexander's pattern number listed within his original text. This will allow you to refer directly to his work if you desire to delve more deeply into Alexander's concepts.

Additionally, each design pattern provides a summary of Alexander's text, describing his concept. This allows you to better understand Alexander's general meaning and intention for the pattern. You will then see **boldfaced text** following each summary; this provides an application of the pattern to an early childhood classroom setting. Finally, photographs of early childhood classrooms accompany each pattern to help you visualize the pattern.

Category 1: Making Connections (General Schemes of Connection)

Within this category, you will find patterns that encourage connectivity. Educators must intentionally promote connections between a child and outside elements found in her world; it is often connections made with peers, with other cultures, and with the earth that enrich a child's life and broaden her awareness. The following patterns address the unique connections that can add depth and breadth to a child's daily experience within his early childhood program.

Play materials should expose children to representations of a variety of cultures, ability levels, genders, and ages.

■ *Mosaic of Cultures (8)*

Ideally, geographical areas support and encourage a mosaic of cultures, allowing each to thrive with its own distinct character, while simultaneously being open and accessible to all other cultures. Many cities are home to coexisting cultural areas, where each reflects its own uniqueness and welcomes the distinctive nature of its neighbors. Everything possible must be done to support and enrich the variety of cultures within a geographical area.

Early childhood programs must adopt a philosophy of acknowledging and celebrating the variety of cultures within the world at large. We live in a global society, and by exposure to a variety of beliefs and practices, children are more likely to grow and develop as citizens who are fully accepting of others. Classroom posters, books, dolls, and other materials must be inclusive of all cultures, as well as all ages and ability levels. Visitors and field trips must also reflect the variety of cultures found within the neighborhood community, as well as around the world.

Consideration for the intimacy gradient within a classroom
intentionally incorporates spaces to accommodate children alone,
in pairs, in small groups, and in larger groups.

■ *Intimacy Gradient (127)*

Whether it is the home or workplace, spaces within a building should be arranged in a sequence corresponding to their degree of privacy. For example, within a home the bedroom is the most intimate space, while the front porch or entrance room is the most public. This "intimacy gradient" allows a person to more easily discern the function and purpose of the space, and to more clearly define the social relationships that are possible within that space. Conversely, if a building has homogeneity of space, whereby every room conveys a similar degree of intimacy, the subtlety of interpersonal relationships is eliminated. Therefore, the spaces in a building must establish an intimacy gradient, creating a sequence that begins at the entrance (the most public part of the space), leading into the slightly more private areas, and finally to the most private domains.

Recognize the intimacy gradient within an early childhood program, allowing for differing shades of meaning and interpersonal relationships. The building entrance should be open and public, a welcoming and open space for all who enter. The offices of the director/administrator are semiprivate, so accommodation must be made for the administrator's privacy, as well as space to provide comfort to visitors, families, and staff.

The classrooms should also contain intimacy gradients, in that there is a need for a common area along with smaller and more enclosed learning center areas. More intimate, private spaces should be provided for children who need a break from the action. Lofts, two-person sofas, and comfy recliner seats are examples of smaller spaces that invite one or two children to sit together. Restrooms should be considered private spaces; allow curtains or enclosures at each restroom stall for those children who require it. Finally, kitchen areas should be semipublic, in that the cooking areas are only open to staff but eating areas are accessible to all—including parent visitors.

The intimacy gradient within this room provides table space for larger groups, open space for small groups to work together within learning centers, loft space that accommodates pairs or small groups above and below, and a relaxing beanbag and small sofa for singles or pairs.

■ *Communal Eating (147)*

Communal eating is a necessary element of group identification and affiliation. Most human societies promote communal eating in order to connect and unite, increasing interpersonal relationships and connections. Therefore, buildings must provide a place where people can eat and come together around food. Groups should make the common meal a priority—an important, comfortable, daily event with room for invited guests.

Early childhood programs should acknowledge the importance of communal eating and the opportunities for growth and development created by such eating. Communal eating fosters social interaction and group affiliation between peers; sitting and conversing with the children also increases critical student-teacher relationships. When meals are served family style, communal eating promotes increasing levels of independence between the children. Treat meals as daily special events and times of relaxation and conversation rather than chores through which you are anxious to rush.

This communal eating space encourages children and adults to "break bread" together, sharing conversations within an aesthetically appealing environment.

Children have been provided with space and a variety of materials to fully engage their creativity and imagination.

■ *Classroom Workshop (157)*

As work becomes more decentralized, moving away from the office and toward more relaxed environments such as the home, a workshop becomes a relevant and important consideration. Therefore, a place where substantial work can be accomplished should be created in the building. The workshop should be given the character and respect of a real workplace, rather than merely a small space set aside for a hobby.

As Maria Montessori promoted, children thrive on real work. Real work is authentic, providing a sense of accomplishment, as well as relevance, within a child's growing sphere of influence. Provide space and materials to pique the children's interest in a variety of activities that encourage focused and sustained effort, combining intellectual curiosity with hands-on activity and a feeling of accomplishment. Such children's work gains its inspiration from adult work, including activities such as woodworking and construction, sewing and knitting, running a store, and so on. Early childhood educators should creatively arrange the space and materials for children's burgeoning real-world efforts.

Smocks and goggles ensure safety as the child practices hammering a nail into the tree stump. A clothespin can provide stability to the nail for the younger learners.

The woodworking area allows young children to experience success as they create their own materials, aided by the teacher. These children drilled holes into bottle caps and wooden circles, and tacked them to pieces of wood to make their own cars.

In the foreground, a piece of Styrofoam is covered with burlap—the perfect material to allow toddlers and young preschoolers to gain practice with a plastic hammer (and golf tees).

■ *Things from Your Life (253)*

Modern décor does not have to be slick or follow a prescribed, acceptable aesthetic that reflects current trends. Interior spaces are most beautiful when reflecting the passions and memories of one's life. Therefore, tastefully share the things you care for and that tell your personal story.

Children create meaning from their environment, and this includes the visual images surrounding them. Stripping their environment of visual reminders of their life—successes, projects, artwork, and photos—removes a critical opportunity for both pride and reflection. The Reggio Emilia philosophy wonderfully reflects this appreciation through the use of documentation. Providing visual reminders of children's recent activities through outcome evidence (drawings, writings, projects), as well as photographic documentation, allows the children to grow socially, emotionally, and cognitively.

The images above show documentation reflecting thoughts and experiences related to children's clay exploration.

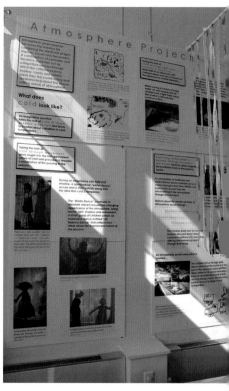

Here, documentation captures the thoughts, artistic representations, and photographs related to a long-term relationship with a local park, as well as the children's efforts to address the problem of littering at the park.

The practice of documentation, found with classrooms inspired by the Reggio Emilia approach, provides visual reminders of current and past projects—things from their lives that represent points of pride for the children, educators, and parents.

A miniature greenhouse promotes a child's connection to the earth, as well as a sense of responsibility for its caretaking.

Exploration opportunities with natural materials allow children to connect to the earth, even in an urban environment.

Nature can be effectively incorporated into a classroom's materials and design.

■ *Connection to the Earth (168)*

A building conveys a sense of isolation unless it is connected to the natural environment around it. Humans have a deep-seated need to have a physical connection to the earth, and this must be reflected in the structures we inhabit. Therefore, connect the building to the earth by interweaving it with the surrounding landscape. Create paths, terraces, steps, gardens, and so forth, extending from the building to any aspects of nature that surround it. When possible, place them so that the boundary between nature and the building is ambiguous, making it difficult to determine where the building ends and the earth begins. Elements to consider include trees, vegetable gardens, gardens growing wild, garden walls or seats, trellised walkways, and composts.

Environmental awareness should be a fundamental part of education for young children; such awareness is severely limited without access to the earth and its resources. Planting, harvesting, and enjoying the bounties of nature accomplish critical intellectual goals for children, incorporating science, math, and language, as well as encouraging a caring disposition. While many urban schools may not have immediate connection to the earth around the perimeter of the building, it is crucial to find ways of establishing such connections. For example, vegetable and flower gardens can be cultivated in pots and placed indoors or outdoors, allowing children to intimately experience the excitement of the life cycle of plants.

Materials found within nature, displayed at the child's level and in an attractive manner, increase a child's connection to the natural environment.

Category 2: Coming and Going (Entrance and Exit)

Times of transition—arriving in the morning and leaving at the end of the day—can be stressful for both parents and children. It is for this reason a close eye should be given to the entrance and exit areas of the early childhood program. Early childhood programs need to be safe havens for families—welcoming them at the start of the day in a calming and homelike atmosphere, reassuring them that a day filled with safety, security, and active engagement lies ahead for their child. Each pattern within this category encourages serious consideration of all aspects of the entrance and exit space, from the street view of the program to the building and classroom entrances.

The building edge of this early childhood program uses lighting, awnings, and landscaping to promote an engaging zone of entry.

■ *Building Edge (160)*

Buildings are typically envisioned as spaces that turn inward; it may seem that the most important part of a building is its interior. This viewpoint leads to buildings that are institutional, isolated, and cut off from their surroundings. However, buildings can also be conceptualized as spaces that are oriented toward the outside as well. This view would include thinking of the building as having a lively "building edge," connected to the social fabric of its surrounding area with benches, balconies, nature, and places to sit or stop. Treat the edge of a building as a place in and of itself—a zone with volume rather than a line or interface with no thickness. Outside of the building, make places with depth and a covering, inviting all to sit, lean, walk, and look onto interesting outdoor life.

Attention to the building edge is often overlooked or superficially addressed with signage and a hanging flower basket or two. An early childhood program should be an integral part of a community and, as such, should project an inviting and engaging zone of entry. Providing partial shelter, along with places to sit, stand, and engage with those coming and going, are key ways of achieving a vibrant and engaging building edge. This will promote the important concept of early childhood programs as places that are equally concerned with indoor and outdoor learning opportunities.

This early childhood program uses decorative elements to welcome visitors.

■ *Entrance Transition (112)*

A building with a graceful transition between the street and its interior is more tranquil than one that opens directly off the street. If at all possible, make a transition space between the street and the front door. Mark it with a change of light, sound, direction, surface, or level—a change of view that allows visitors to visually and mentally transition from the street to the building.

The entrance transition between the street and building should offer community members—both clients and visitors—an inviting and welcoming change from the impersonality of the surrounding area. The addition of welcoming signage, plants/ nature, appropriate sounds, and warm lighting are all ways to set the building apart from its surroundings and represent quality early childhood programming.

The wooden pergola, landscaping, and walkway provide an effective transition space between the street and front door of this early childhood program.

Ideally, a reception area should be aesthetically pleasing, welcoming all who enter with eye-catching information about the life of the program. Offering umbrellas to borrow on a rainy day is a practical and thoughtful addition.

■ *Welcoming Reception (149)*

First impressions are critical. Once a visitor passes through the entrance transition, she will encounter the inner reception area of the building—a visitor's first impression of the building's staff and services. Therefore, provide a welcoming area immediately inside the entrance—a soft seating area, warm lighting, and food and coffee if possible. The reception desk should not act as a barrier between the visitors and the receptionist or administrator, but rather be placed to one side to facilitate a warm greeting.

Welcoming all who enter is both good business practice and a sign of a quality educational environment. Be sure that the entrance and reception area send the right message about the quality of care provided at your program—welcoming, informative, and suited to each child's needs. Welcoming children as they enter is critically important for their social and emotional well-being and lets them know they are valued members of the school community.

■ *Entrance Room (130)*

The entrance room is an important space that one passes through to enter or leave the building. Proper attention to this area acknowledges the importance of providing a specific space to say hello or good-bye; a clearly delineated greeting/exit space eases the process for all involved. Therefore, in addition to the elements mentioned previously, things to consider for the entrance room are the relationship of windows to the entrance (a means of seeing those who are entering the building is preferred); the need for shelter outside the door (a covered area is both welcoming and useful in inclement weather); the interior standing/sitting area (comfy seating, warm lighting, etc.); and the space for shoes, coats, and so on.

Within the context of early childhood programs, the concept of the entrance room applies to the entrance of the school, as well as to the entrance into each classroom. As mentioned previously, welcoming items should be an integral part of the entrance and reception areas of the school. Likewise, each classroom should have distinctive elements within its entrance that identify the classroom's special qualities, staff, and children. Provide a distinct point at which the children can more easily separate from their families in the morning and where visitors and families can receive updated information (written information, daily journals, photos, mementos, etc.) regarding the ongoing life of the classroom.

The inviting *décor* of this entrance room provides a cozy space for interacting upon entering and exiting the school.

An open and airy entrance room, strategically placed prior to entering the heart of the school, promotes personal interaction and relationships.

This attractive entrance room acknowledges the importance of a defined greeting/exit space that invites conversation among children, parents, and visitors.

Category 3: On the Move! (Circulation)

Space management is a key consideration when improving your pedagogy through spatial considerations. Effectively managing the spaces within a school aids in the movement through and between classrooms, which in turn can maximize student learning and relationship building. The ease of one's flow through the space can determine the level of focused attention (or frustration) experienced by children as they go about their day.

Providing open space between classroom furniture and learning centers reduces traffic congestion within a room.

■ *Flow through Rooms (131)*

The movement or circulation space between and within rooms is equally important as the rooms themselves. The circulation space, whether generous or narrow, seriously impacts the social interactions within the rooms. Therefore, consider the generosity of movement between the rooms and within the rooms. Delineate areas within the room according to the intimacy gradient and the logical flow of traffic.

Study the traffic patterns currently in place and be alert to the flow of teachers and children through each classroom. Make note of children's arguments over space and use that as a cue to rethink the flow within the room. Does the current placement of learning areas allow for a logical circulation? Do the children have enough space to move between areas without interrupting one another's play? Use common sense to place wet activities near a water source and noisy activities away from quiet reading corners. Be aware of the flow to and from the children's personal spaces (lockers, cubbies, etc.) so that the children can go to their personal space without interrupting groups of playing children.

Space for children to work should be large enough to reduce overcrowding yet small enough to allow for shared use of materials, promoting the comfortable feeling that arises from a defined play space.

■ *Short Passages (132)*

Passages between rooms must be treated as if they were rooms in and of themselves. Long, institutional corridors are often sterile and representative of bureaucracy and monotony. Such corridors often lack in comfort and beauty, and are viewed as just a means to get from one room to another. Therefore, when possible, keep the passages between rooms short and reduce their scale by making them as much like rooms as possible. Make them generous in shape and light; use furniture, bookshelves, seating areas, and warm (or natural) lighting to deinstitutionalize the building passages.

Take an unbiased look at the corridors in your school. Do they give a warm and welcoming vibe? Are they homelike and pleasant or institutional and monotonous? The corridors may not directly impact the children's learning, but a pleasant flow through a building adds to the experience that all have within—from children and staff to families and visitors. Add furnishings (chairs, tables, bookshelves, artwork) and lighting within the passages or corridors to promote a sense of beauty and comfort, as well as to add to the usable space within the school.

Hallways and stairways can be decorated to celebrate childhood, as well as to showcase student work.

Corridors between classrooms can be treated as useful
learning spaces rather than empty, sterile passageways.

Category 4: Let the Sunshine In! (Lighting and Color)

The lighting and color of a room can project an immediate ambience and atmosphere. Rooms can seem warm and cozy or cold and institutional, based on lighting and color alone. Attention paid to the various aspects of this category can inspire positive room transformation, benefiting both teachers and children alike.

Classroom design should take advantage of the human propensity for light and shed lots of natural light onto the learning environment.

■ *Indoor Sunlight (128)*

By nature, humans are drawn toward brightness (Ginthner 2004). Most of us long for rooms that are bathed in natural light, rather than windowless spaces containing only artificial lighting. Very few aspects of a room are as meaningful as a sun-filled space. Therefore, do not minimize the importance of indoor sunlight. A room with natural light can make the difference between a room that is warm, bright, and inviting rather than cold, dark, and gloomy.

If possible, provide indoor sunlight in all areas and classrooms to meet the human need for natural light—this would apply to both the children and adults in the school. When the building does not have this capability, pay particular attention to providing pools of light (see next page).

Decorative elements within the classroom can highlight natural light, providing a sparkle and shine to the space.

■ *Pools of Light (252)*

Uniform illumination is meant to make the light in a room as flat and even as possible in a mistaken effort to imitate daylight. However, the light outdoors is rarely even, with variations of light that change from place to place with the ever-changing position of the sun. Additionally, as social spaces are often defined by light, uniform illumination can be detrimental to the social nature of a space. Therefore, place lights low and position them strategically near social gathering spaces. Such placement will form individual pools of light, encompassing the chairs and tables and reinforcing the social character of such spaces.

Evaluate the lighting sources in your classrooms and corridors. If possible, use overhead fluorescent lighting sparingly. Supplement fluorescent lighting with hanging lights, floor lamps, table lamps, track lighting—whatever is possible to create pools of light focused on social spaces. Colored lamp shades and hanging lights can reinforce a warm glow. Use beading, strings of minilights, and a variety of effects to add interest and character to each room.

Light tables and mirrors provide pools of light that draw children and add character to the room.

Nontraditional overhead lights provide greater variations and pools of light, aided by softening fabric that is hung from above.

Without the use of flat, overhead fluorescent lighting, those in the space can better appreciate the pools of light provided by windows, lamps, and creative hanging lights.

Small spaces can become more inviting when lamps provide pools of light.

A tapestry of light, where the classroom is not dependent on uniform fluorescent lights, adds to the interest and texture of the room.

Using a mixture of lamps, light tables, and hanging lights creates a varied tapestry of light within the classroom space.

■ Tapestry of Light and Dark (135)

Generally, the most effective settings for work, play, or living are characterized by light. Buildings with uniform light levels are uninspiring and ineffective, denying our tendency to gravitate toward sunlight. Since light places can only be defined by contrasting them with darker ones, nonuniformity of light within a room is most desirable. Therefore, create "tapestries of light and dark" within rooms, alternating pools of light with less lit spaces. Be sure to light important social spaces to create a distinctive tapestry of light and dark.

While areas for children cannot be dark due to safety considerations, it is nonetheless important to pay attention to the variation of light within rooms and between rooms. Concentrate lighting on socially important spaces, acknowledging humans' natural tendencies to gather near light. Use a variety of lamps and colorizing and softening techniques to make a room seem less institutional and to add to its distinctive nature.

The natural lighting and cheery color palate heighten
the warmth of a space.

■ *Warm Colors (250)*

Institutional buildings often seem depressing and cold because of their color palette—pale greens and grays. Conversely, interiors filled with natural woods and bright colors feel warm and comfortable. Interestingly, it is not the actual color of a surface that makes a place warm or cold, but rather the color of the light—the complex interaction between the color of the light sources and the way the light bounces on and off the surfaces. Therefore, choose surface colors that, in combination with the color of a room's natural, artificial, and reflected lighting, create a warm glow.

Note the warmth of the colors and light within each room. Generally, yellows, reds, oranges, and browns create a warmer feel than blues, greens, and grays. The overall feeling of a room should create a warm and inviting mood for all who interact in the space. This is easier to achieve in a room that contains more natural sunlight, but it can also be enhanced by the choice of lighting and surface colors.

Nontraditional lighting allows for a warm interplay with the natural woods and vivid colors used in the room.

Category 5: A Place of My Own
(Room Structure)

Many aspects of room structure contribute to the individual character of a room. The patterns listed within this category can appeal to each person differently, allowing each to find her own niche within the larger classroom space. Providing spaces for children to call their own leads to positive emotional responses that can promote learning.

This "common area at the heart" is a flexible, multiuse space that allows siblings and children of different ages to play and spend time with one another.

A common room that houses a wide variety of artistic media allows for a change of space outside of the child's usual classroom.

Corridors between rooms can also serve as common areas, providing additional space for playful exploration.

■ *Common Areas at the Heart (129)*

Social groups are formed and sustained by regular contact among members. As referenced by the intimacy gradient, areas that are common are public spaces located at the "heart" of the building (or room) where individuals can gather for a variety of purposes. Therefore, ensure that there is a common area for *every* social group. The common area should be at the heart or center of activity for the group.

Common areas are a typical addition within early childhood classrooms; they are places where all the children within the classroom can gather comfortably. Common areas should be suitable for multiple uses and flexible enough to be shifted and adjusted to accommodate a variety of needs. Less frequent are designated common areas for other groups associated with early childhood programs—staff, parents, and members of the community. Private common areas for staff promote group affiliation and build relationships. Such areas could also be offered for use by parent and community groups, which will help convey that the school is a relevant community asset.

This common area sits between four classrooms, allowing children to play with friends in other rooms.

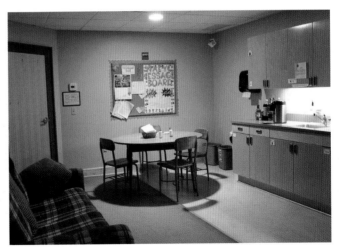

Common areas for educators are also important, serving as areas that promote camaraderie, collaboration, and conviviality.

■ *A Space of One's Own (141)*

While group affiliation and connection are critically important, people also need the space and opportunity to be alone. Providing a special, individualized space of one's own sends the message that each child is an important member of the group and is allowed the opportunity to individualize his own space and personal territory. Therefore, set aside a personal spot for each member of the group, located at the far end of the intimacy gradient—away from the common spaces.

Within any school, each child should be given a personal space of his own—a place to put his coat, shoes, and personal belongings. This space should also allow a child to display his individuality via items of his choosing. Photographs of family, favorite art projects, and decorative elements promote a child's sense of ownership over that small space he can call his own. Likewise, staff members should be provided a personal space of their own—one that reflects their individuality and allows them to safely store personal items.

Each child is provided space for personal items carried to and from home; mailboxes and bulletin boards assist in maintaining open communication with parents.

A small mudroom provides a passage between the hallway and classroom; this allows for storage of personal items and facilitates the ease of transitioning between outdoor gear and the indoor learning space.

Child-sized furniture aids in classroom flexibility, allowing the educators to adjust the size of learning areas to accommodate differing classroom needs.

■ *Flexible Classroom Space (146)*

Every organization faces the need for change, and the working space of a building or room should be able to accommodate such change. Therefore, provide the means to create a variety of spaces that satisfy differing spatial needs. Arrange the spaces so people can work in smaller groups and larger groups, with the potential for contact with others as well as privacy.

When considering the flow through rooms, pay particular attention to the flexibility of the arrangement of space. To allow for extreme flexibility, use a variety of movable furniture—shelving units, sitting spaces, carts, partitions, or other safe yet unique pieces—to differentiate between learning center areas. Another option is to differentiate the space from above—by hanging fabric and blinds from the ceiling, for example—to flexibly delineate one area from another.

Hanging fixtures or dividers, like the fabric seen here, allow for cost-effective and flexible differentiation of classroom space. Open metal shelving units also encourage space differentiation while allowing for clear visibility.

■ *Window Place (180)*

Humans innately love "window places"; such places should not be viewed as mere luxuries. Humans' love for window places is intuitive, based on the desire to sit and be comfortable, as well as the tendency we have to be drawn toward light. In every room, find ways to creatively use at least one window by making it into a window place. Use a variety of seating options along with a flat surface (shelf, cabinet, etc.) on which select items can be placed.

For children, window places accommodate two basic needs—to follow their instinct to be drawn toward light and to satisfy their curiosity to see the outside world. At least one window in each room should be a window place, arranged to accommodate the developmental needs of children. Very young children should be provided a space to be seated at window height. Toddlers should have safe (padded or carpeted) stairs or sturdy standing stools to allow them to look out. Preschool children should be provided with a comfy chair or stool to view outdoor activities. School-age children should have a couch or group seating to enable them to socialize at the window place.

The window enhances the cozy feel of the reading area by utilizing natural light and the warmth of the sun.

A grouping of comfy seating options, placed strategically near a window, acknowledges humans' natural preference for light.

This mulberry tree provides a unique outdoor child cave.

Hanging strips of fabric from above can safely differentiate small spaces.

This loft area is small enough to accommodate one to three children, providing a child-sized space to engage in imaginative play.

The area under a loft can be transformed into a semiprivate space for young learners.

The men's ties outlining the perimeter of this child cave ensures safe monitoring of the child.

■ *Child Caves (203)*

Children find tiny, cave-like play spaces irresistible. Just as infants enjoy being swaddled and held close, young children have an innate need to be enclosed in a space that is just their size. Therefore, create spaces that satisfy this need for a small enclosure. If possible, tuck them away in natural leftover spaces, such as under stairs, counters, lofts, and tables. Keep ceiling heights low (two and a half to four feet) and entrances small.

As always, safety is the first concern when planning early childhood spaces. It is totally possible, however, to combine the requirement of safe monitoring of activities with a child's craving for small spaces. Creatively address a young child's need to play in small spaces by finding appropriate places in each classroom; fashion "walls" out of materials such as gauzy fabric, narrow strips of cloth, or beads. Such materials permit cave-like play without hindering adult supervision. Leaving one side of the cave open also allows for ease of supervision.

■ *Bulk Storage (145)*

All buildings require a bulk storage space where items that are needed only periodically can be stored. Therefore, place bulk storage spaces in extra, out-of-the-way places in the building—in attics, under stairs, or in sheds.

All schools need space for bulk storage, along with room for everyday storage. Find a place to keep bulk items that are only used sparingly or materials that you rotate seasonally. Be sure to dispose of items that haven't been used in three years or more! Careful consideration must be given to daily storage requirements—cabinets for art supplies and items that are for teachers' use only. Locked storage, out of the reach of children, must be provided for items that are toxic or dangerous.

Storage rooms allow for circulation of classroom items, thereby increasing engagement as children are regularly exposed to different play materials.

Outdoor storage facilitates a variety of active experiences outside the confines of the classroom.

A separate room is used for
bulk storage of small craft
items, allowing for easy
access when ready to be
used under adult supervision.

Category 6: Be Comfortable (Seating)

At home, people often have a favorite couch or chair they enjoy—a well-deserved respite at the end of a long day. Unfortunately, seating within schools is often neither restful nor individualized and can seem institutional and uninviting. This category prompts reflection on the many moods chairs can evoke and the purposes they can serve.

Loft areas offer a variety of seating options, both over and under.

■ *Sequence of Sitting Spaces (142)*

Every inch of a building has the potential to be a great sitting space. Ideally, the desired levels of comfort and intimacy should dictate the differing seating arrangements offered. Therefore, in conjunction with the intimacy gradient of the room and building, create a variety of sitting spaces that are sequenced according to their degree of intimacy and enclosure. A continuum of sitting spaces, from the most public (outdoor and entrance) to the most private (singular spots for private time) are desirable.

Offer a complete variety of sitting spaces throughout the school, within the corridors and in each classroom. Equip the spaces so that a variety of needs can be met, including one's need to sit alone, in pairs, in small groups, or in a large group. Be aware of the levels of intimacy provided by each seating arrangement and provide for all levels—from small individual chairs and comfy recliners, to couches or small groupings of chairs, to group tables or rugs.

A sequence of outdoor sitting spaces allows for any number of educators and friends to enjoy rest, relaxation, and conversation within a natural environment.

Consideration of a sequence of sitting spaces intentionally provides cozy, small spaces for one or two children, as well as a variety of seating options for small to large groups of children.

▪ Different Chairs (251)

People's moods and personalities can be reflected in the chairs in which they choose to sit. Whether they are big comfy chairs, stools, or rocking chairs, each type of chair satisfies a different mood or need at any given time. Therefore, choose a variety of different chairs to place throughout the building—the variations are endless. Consider chairs that are big and small, old and new, soft and hard, rockers and gliders, with arms and without, and made of various materials, such as wicker, wood, and cloth.

Providing for a variety of seating options adds to the rich experience to be had within an early childhood program. All too often, chair options within early childhood schools are uniform and hard plastic, which disregards the importance of matching one's mood to one's seating preference. The experience of a child, teacher, family member, or visitor is enriched when exposed to a multitude of seating possibilities, allowing for many different types of social interactions or individualized and personal encounters.

Be on the lookout for unique options: claw-footed bathtubs, cast-off stadium seats, and wooden stumps are examples of repurposed seating that can add character and interest to a room.

A reading corner, placed near natural light and incorporating both hard and soft seating options, promotes relaxation and interaction as the children enjoy their selections.

Providing differing types of chairs, with variations in size, firmness, and materials, allows children to express their moods and seating preferences at any given point during the day.

Sofas promote teacher-to-student and student-to-student bonding.

Wide, carpeted stairs
leading to an upper
play area provide
plenty of space to play
or sit safely.

■ *Stair Seats (125)*

People seem to gravitate toward spaces where they are high enough to oversee what is happening and low enough to be close to the action. Therefore, stair seats and variations thereof (seats at the bottom of lofts, large step stools, counter stools, or low outdoor seats, for example) are all desirable seating options that allow people to sit and watch the existing activities and events.

Recognize children's need to sit and watch activities in multiple places and at multiple levels. While maintaining an eye on safety, build or provide stair-type places, perhaps with different widths, for children to sit together. Stair seats provide a unique and appealing vantage point and experience as opposed to simply sitting on the floor or in a chair.

Stair seats near a window provide an appealing vantage point for standing or sitting.

Category 7: Take It Outside! (Outdoor Spaces)

In the hustle-bustle world we inhabit, with its ever-present emphasis on technology, children are experiencing less time outdoors than ever before. In many primary schools, recess is being replaced by longer spans of time in the classroom; after school, children are increasingly participating in structured team sports and activities. There is a great need for reintroducing children to the simplicity of the outdoors, reconnecting them with the beauty and wonder of the natural world. Time outside encourages creativity, problem solving, health and wellness, among other things; anything done inside can also be done outside, to the great delight of children. The patterns below prompt reflective consideration of the many ways children can participate in activities that are out of doors.

This adventure playground area uses natural, raw materials along with added play items to immerse children in creative activities.

Children are inventors, creators, and collaborators when provided the space and raw materials to bring their creations to life.

■ *Adventure Playground (73)*

Children invariably prefer creating their own elaborate structures—castles, towns, creative buildings—out of cartons, rocks, and dead branches, rather than playing with structures that are permanent and inflexible. Essentially, playground structures emerged from the imaginations of playground designers, supplanting the need for children's inventive and inspired creations. As a result, children adopt a less desirable, more passive role when only clean, safe, yet unimaginative playground structures are used. Therefore, establish a separate playground area that is not stylized but contains raw materials of all kinds—boxes, barrels, nets, simple tools, frames, grass, and water—where children can create and re-create adventures that were conceived within their own minds.

In the interest of style and safety, the majority of American playgrounds have removed most opportunities for creativity. Providing raw materials of all sorts, while possibly less stylish to the outside observer, allows children to fully engage their imaginations, putting themselves into a world of their own invention. While keeping an eye on state licensing requirements and safety, look for creative ways to provide a true adventure playground space for children. By doing so, children are challenged to cultivate their own innovative and productive ideas for play rather than solely being subjected to the imagination of others.

This playground made use of the current topography to create a natural space for a slide.

Combining a water pump and hollowed logs with a natural sloping topography encourages fun scientific exploration.

To make the best use of space, the children's garden is nestled among the restful hammocks.

■ *Half-Hidden Garden (111)*

Building a garden is an important way to promote our connection to the earth. A garden, whether it contains flowers or fruits and vegetables, connects one to the earth the way nothing else can. The preferred location of a garden is half hidden—not too public and close to the street and not too isolated where it won't be seen or used. Therefore, provide a garden area that is partially exposed to passersby as well as partially private and hidden.

Planting, caring for, and harvesting a school garden offers priceless opportunities for children's collaboration and learning. Cross-curricular opportunities abound, from discussing the life cycle (science) to counting seeds (math) and reading stories about the outdoors (literacy). The entire garden could be cared for by all students equally; alternatively, it could be apportioned so that each classroom adopts and cares for different segments of the space. Regardless of the method, planting and caring for a garden holds countless opportunities for teaching and learning among young children and adults.

Urban settings can incorporate container gardening opportunities for children.

Gardens can provide a multitude of cross-curricular opportunities, from literacy (labeling the plants, increasing vocabulary) to science (learning about the life cycle, caring for living things).

■ *Outdoor Classroom (163)*

An outdoor room, while not providing the extremely intimate experience with nature as afforded by a garden, fulfills an equally important need for spending time outdoors. The benefit of an outdoor room is to encourage similar activities experienced within an indoor room, yet with the added benefit of the sun, wind, smells, sounds, and textures unique to the outdoors. Therefore, provide a place outdoors that has the characteristics of an enclosed room, taking on the feeling of a room while still being open to the sky.

The outdoor room should be distinctly different from either the playground or the garden. Each type of outdoor space has different purposes and advantages; therefore, each should be given equal amounts of respect and attention. The provision of an outdoor room allows teachers to engage in similar types of hands-on learning activities that occur indoors, but with the advantages of being outside. The outdoor room could be in the same location as the playground and the garden but should be differentiated through the use of movable enclosures and furniture, simulating an outdoor classroom.

While not enclosed, this space effectively serves as an outdoor classroom, differentiated from the surrounding area by a ceiling and floor. A picnic table provides opportunities for bringing learning activities out of doors.

The gazebo provides an attractive and covered outdoor classroom space.

This version of an outdoor classroom provides a differentiated space
to enjoy artistic self-expression activities.

The classroom door
provides a direct
connection to the
outdoor play area.

■ *Opening to the Street (165)*

A connection to the world beyond a building is best facilitated by offering a large and accessible opening to the street. When one can clearly see the interior space from the street and vice versa, one's world is enlarged and enriched. Such a connection allows for greater possibilities for communication and learning and for a broadened horizon. Therefore, where possible, create an opening to the street that is large, visible, and accessible. There are three basic options: (1) visible access to the outdoors—a glass wall or large glass windows facing the outside; (2) partial physical access to the outdoors—an outdoor-facing wall that offers partial access via a large window, shutters, half wall, etc.; (3) full physical access to the outdoors—an outdoor-facing wall that can totally open, providing a means for activity to cross paths from the inside to the outside. Full physical access to the outdoors could be aided by a sliding wall or sliding door, a garage door, a large door opening, or any means whereby the outdoor wall can be eliminated for a period of time. The third option is most ideal, since it invites a continuous flow between inside and outside.

Providing for an intimate connection to the outdoors greatly increases the opportunities for teaching and learning. Connection to green spaces and the benefits of nature are greatly enhanced, as are opportunities to build on hands-on learning activities. The optimal case would be to provide an opening that can eliminate the barrier between the indoor space and the outdoor space, where activities can flow from indoors to outdoors and vice versa. Obviously, safety concerns imply that the outdoor area be walled to guarantee that children remain within the confines of the classroom.

This classroom provides immediate and safe access to the fenced outdoor playground.

Applying What You've Learned

Each of these patterns was originally intended for architects as a means of aiding their understanding of and language about important aspects of building and room design. As an early childhood educator, you are now "in the know"—enlightened in ways in which you can use architectural patterns to enhance your classroom space.

Using a discerning eye regarding your classroom or school, along with your newfound understanding, how can you enhance the children's experience within the space? Part 3, "Design Patterns Tool Kits: Applying What You've Learned" will help you apply this knowledge. This part of the book provides concrete ways for you to evaluate and transform your existing classroom into one that is brimming with character and individuality.

You've been inspired by the ideas and photographs found within this text, and now you're ready to make a change. Where do you begin?

Part 3 of this book provides you with the tools necessary to reframe your thinking and make changes that will greatly improve the space that you and the children under your care inhabit on a daily basis. The *Ready, Set, Go!* toolbox described below will help you create a vision for change—where to start, what to do, who you can call on for help, and so on. This broad and comprehensive toolbox includes smaller, more defined tool kits that will help narrow your vision, compartmentalizing your task into more manageable parts.

The first tool kit, *Ready*, is intended to help you analyze your current situation; the second, *Set*, provides suggestions for brainstorming new ideas; and the final tool kit, *Go!*, shares practical advice for implementing your new designs. Within each of the *Ready, Set, Go!* tool kits, you will discover tips and suggestions to help you reconstruct your classroom space into one that is both engaging and inspiring.

Ready, Set, Go!

The *Ready, Set, Go!* toolbox provides you with all that is necessary to think deeply about your physical environment and to make it more effective.

- *Ready*: tools to analyze what you have—Reframe, Recruit, Record
- *Set*: tools to brainstorm what you need—Story, Spark, Segment
- *Go!*: tools to implement what you want to achieve—Go What? Go How? Go When? Go Again

■ *Tool Kit #1: Ready:* **Reframe, Recruit, Record**

Before you can make any changes to your classroom, it is important to take a close look at what you already have. What is the present state of your classroom environment? Are you pleased with the room arrangement, learning materials, and design aesthetic? Is it possible you may be desensitized to its current condition? Can you try to look at the space as if you were an outsider? Consider the following tools that will help you be ready for change.

REFRAME

Reframe what you see within the space. As humans, we build on prior knowledge and continuously add new information to that which we've experienced. We understand the world by continuously comparing things that are new to things that we've already experienced—constructing new meanings from everything that happened before. This tendency makes learning more streamlined, which is very helpful in most situations. However, this also causes you to see your environment within the context of previous experience—just as you've always seen it.

An awareness of this human tendency is critical to the process of environmental change. Just as you place your favorite photo in the center of a picture frame, you also view your classroom as you've always seen it. *Reframe your visual information*—look at your classroom space differently. Metaphorically shift your "picture frame" to gain a new perspective. Stand on a table to see the room from above. Kneel in order to see the room from the perspective of a child. Look through a window to visualize it from the outside. Reframe the space from all angles. It is only when you free your mind from preconceived visualizations that you are able to start from scratch and make changes.

RECRUIT

Recruit individuals to join in your efforts. You cannot do this alone. Change can be scary; it is for this reason that meaningful change can rarely be sustained when using a top-down approach. Changes to the environment must result from grassroots efforts, with buy-in from all the stakeholders.

Find others who are passionate about room design, or at the very least, interested in pedagogical improvements. Share your ideas, your vision, and your passion. Share what you've learned in this book. Gain feedback and support from other educators, as well as children, parents, and community members. Parents and community members can prove to be wonderful resources not only for ideas and support but also for donations of supplies and furnishings. Teaching is often an isolated profession where one plans and implements without assistance from others; however, if environmental change is to be successful and sustained, it must be undertaken by all.

RECORD

Record evidence that will aid in your analysis. A key tool of analysis consists of self-study through objective data collection. Without substantive and meaningful data, it will be difficult for you to gauge your current status and proceed confidently. Ideas for objective data gathering can include the following:

Photography. Take photos of the room from many angles. Your brain interprets items in print differently than what you see in real life. Your brain also tends to ignore things that are commonplace or typical. While this tendency helps your brain operate more efficiently and prevents overstimulation, it is not helpful when performing a room analysis. It is possible to ignore little annoyances or even large problems when you see them every day. It is easier to gain a more objective stance, however, when looking at a photograph. Pin your photographs to poster board and look at them with fresh eyes. You are sure to see your room design in a new way.

Floor Plans. Draw a floor plan of the room and have others who inhabit the space do the same. Determine what each person's floor plan includes (and does not include) and what items are the same. Everyone will probably include the areas perceived to be the most important. These drawings will stimulate discussion regarding perceptions of room design and materials. What is critical to include in the room? What is simply taken for granted? Engage in the tough discussions regarding

the items included in the space, along with the arrangement of the space to determine which items are developmentally appropriate, inquiry based, and aesthetically pleasing.

Room and Materials Analysis. Undertake an objective analysis of the areas and materials used most often in your room. Write down the learning centers within the room, and for a one-hour time span, tally the numbers of children within each area (or those merely wandering throughout the room). Note which materials are used. Undertake this exercise at different times of the day and on different days of the week. Swap places with teachers in other rooms for an even more detached analysis of room activity. Such forms of self-study will aid in an unbiased view of the most popular spaces and materials within the room. Meet as a group to discuss your findings, and cross-examine the data. Any such effort promises to bring a greater level of understanding and will guide you toward the next steps in the process of change.

■ *Tool Kit #2: Set:* Story, Spark, Segment

Once you have undertaken an objective self-study of your classroom space, you are ready to dig into the next tool kit. The *Set* tool kit consists of ways of generating new ideas, using the data you've collected to identify ways in which your space can be transformed. The following tools will *set* you on the mark, positioning you on the brink of change.

STORY

Your classroom should tell a story, with children as the protagonists. If you could use your classroom space to tell your dream story, what would that be? Would your classroom tell a story of love and togetherness? Would it tell a mystery? Maybe an action-and-adventure story or one filled with fantasy and imagination? Let your imagination freely express your dreams and desires for all that you want to take place in your classroom, and record these. For each desired story, think about how your classroom could showcase that story. Brainstorm classroom transformation ideas with your colleagues; share your ideal classroom stories and ways that your room could promote love and togetherness, mystery, action and adventure, fantasy, realism, or anything else that you have conceived.

For example, a story filled with fantasy and imagination could use decorative elements such as gauzy fabric and strings of twinkling lights to create the right mood. You can provide many types of dress-up clothes and a stage for children's fantasy plays.

SPARK

Help one another light the spark of creativity as you come up with great ideas. As a group, provide each person with self-stick notes and ask them to write down their wildest dreams and wishes for the classroom space. This is an exercise free of judgment—no idea is out-of-bounds. Hang the idea notes on the wall or on large flip charts. Share all ideas and look at common themes. Categorize the notes according to theme. Finally, within each category, rank the ideas in order of feasibility. Be creative and consider all options for feasibility; often volunteer assistance or donations can help turn a dream into a reality.

SEGMENT

After brainstorming your ideal classroom stories and lighting the spark of your dream classroom design, organize your wishes using the categories found in part 2 of this book. Segmenting and dividing your wishes into categories will allow you to prioritize between wants and needs. Which ideas can be implemented easily and without much cost? Which ideas are more complex, requiring more financial or human resources? This task will lead to your feasibility continuum, explained in the *Go What?* section that follows.

To aid in the task of segmenting your ideas, you may want to use the Design Patterns for Early Childhood Classrooms Worksheet found in the appendix. This can be photocopied and distributed to aid in a clear articulation of the needs and dreams you have for your classroom.

■ *Tool Kit #3: Go!: Go What? Go How? Go When? Go Again*

You have examined your program and brainstormed ideas using Tool Kits 1 and 2, *Ready* and *Set*. Now you're ready to make the changes necessary to enhance your program.

GO WHAT?

The first tool you will need as you take action is a feasibility continuum. After you follow the suggestions in the previous tool kit—brainstorming ideas and placing them into categories—you will order them into a continuum, from the lowest-hanging fruit to the most complex. Which of your ideas are immediately feasible? Which are slightly more involved yet feasible within a reasonable amount of time and minimal effort? And which are more feasible over the long term, requiring much more funding and time? Plans such as room rearrangements, adding pools of light with lamps, and adding multicultural materials can be undertaken immediately with the help of the teachers and children who inhabit the space. Other practical wishes, such as planting gardens, purchasing

a variety of unique seating options, and converting areas into child caves may take a bit more time and effort. Dreams such as indoor lofts, outdoor classrooms, and adventure playgrounds are obviously longer-term goals that must be analyzed in light of budgetary constraints.

Write these items on a large, visible continuum, such as poster board, and post in the teachers' common area for all to see. Also consider typing a professional-looking feasibility continuum to post in your entrance area. This may spur parents to offer materials or assistance as necessary.

GO HOW?

The second tool you will need in the *Go!* tool kit is a task distribution chart. Using your feasibility continuum, determine which stakeholder can help to make each goal a reality. Remember to include all stakeholders when considering the distribution of tasks.

- **Fellow teachers** can help one another realize a vision for the classroom. Each classroom vision may be different, but tasks can be assigned based on talents and skills, thereby helping all to work together and usher in substantive change.
- **Children** can be valuable helpers when given an important task to perform and praised for their success.

- **Parents** may have assets of which you are unaware; post your feasibility continuum to publicize your efforts, and regularly notify the parents through your parent newsletter or special notes home, providing short lists of needed items or services. Parents will surely be pleased in your efforts toward improvement, and you may be surprised at the materials and services they are willing to share.
- **Community stakeholders** should also be tapped for their potential. Similarly to parents, business and community members may be able to assist in your improvements with only a written request to do so. This will also aid in your public relations efforts, making your program a more visible and vital part of the community.

GO WHEN?

The third tool that is required in the *Go!* tool kit is a timeline. Once each room change is identified for feasibility and the responsibilities are distributed among those asked to assist, a timeline can serve the crucial function of keeping everyone on task. A teacher's life is filled with daily events and surprises, and time seems to fly—before you can blink an eye, the school year is coming to an end. For this reason, delineating the changes and when they will happen is vital for success. Having a vision can only take you

so far; it is holding yourself accountable within a certain time frame and striving to accomplish each item by its deadline that turns one's vision into reality. Add this timeline to the feasibility continuum chart for all to see, and agree to hold one another accountable for completing each task in a timely manner.

GO AGAIN

The fourth and final tool involves assessment and reevaluation. Just as we present content to children during a lesson and assess their achievement afterward, the same applies to a transformation of the physical environment. Its success must continuously be assessed and refinements made following each reevaluation.

Following a major classroom alteration, pay close attention to the effects the changes have on others. The children will react to the change, either positively or negatively. Likewise, the teachers may need time to adjust. A word of warning, however: change can be difficult, so all those involved must agree to give each major adaptation a minimum of two weeks (preferably a month) before evaluating its success and making any further substantive changes (or discarding the change altogether). Any change will take time to become ingrained, and just because some children are reacting negatively does not always mean the change is bad. It is your job to model appropriate behavior and to provide encouraging guidance as the children adjust to the change. Some alterations may require several small iterations before finding the proper balance, but the success or failure of transitions is often dependent on the teacher's positive or negative attitude.

Space can be a powerful pedagogical tool, and your desire for change must match the needs of the children within your care. Some children adapt to change very well while others find it thoroughly disconcerting. As an expert on the development of each child in your care, you must gauge the number of classroom conversions that occur within a span of time. Only adopt the number of changes to which your students can calmly and reasonably adjust; after a few weeks, reevaluate the change and exclusively introduce a new variation only after the students have successfully adapted to the previous one.

Pedagogy and Space within Your Classroom

The tools presented here are intended to spark your imagination and provide many opportunities to reflect and reimagine your current classroom space. Joined with the design patterns and example classrooms reflected in part 2, this text provides you with both design inspirations and concrete suggestions for an enhanced early childhood space—one that is functional, developmentally appropriate, and aesthetically pleasing to all who enter.

Name(s): _____
_____
Date: _____

Within each of the seven categories below, assess the bulleted patterns. On the line next to each pattern, list your points of pride and areas of need. Determine which needs can be more immediately fulfilled and which dreams will take more resources and planning. Keep track of these in the spaces provided below.

Category 1: Making Connections (General Schemes of Connection)
- Mosaic of Cultures _____
- Intimacy Gradient _____
- Communal Eating _____
- Classroom Workshop _____
- Things from Your Life _____
- Connection to the Earth _____

Specific Needs for Now: _____
Dreams for the Future: _____

Category 2: Coming and Going (Entrance and Exit)
- Building Edge _____
- Entrance Transition _____
- Welcoming Reception _____
- Entrance Room _____

Specific Needs for Now: _____
Dreams for the Future: _____

Category 3: On the Move! (Circulation)
- Flow through Rooms _____
- Short Passages _____

Specific Needs for Now: _____
Dreams for the Future: _____

Category 4: Let the Sunshine In! *(Lighting and Color)*

- Indoor Sunlight _____
- Pools of Light _____
- Tapestry of Light and Dark _____
- Warm Colors _____

Specific Needs for Now: _____

Dreams for the Future: _____

Category 5: A Place of My Own *(Room Structure)*

- Common Areas at the Heart _____
- A Space of One's Own _____
- Flexible Classroom Space _____
- Window Place _____
- Child Caves _____
- Bulk Storage _____

Specific Needs for Now: _____

Dreams for the Future: _____

Category 6: Be Comfortable *(Seating)*

- Sequence of Sitting Spaces _____
- Different Chairs _____
- Stair Seats _____

Specific Needs for Now: _____

Dreams for the Future: _____

Category 7: Take It Outside! *(Outdoor Spaces)*

- Adventure Playground _____
- Half-Hidden Garden _____
- Outdoor Classroom _____
- Opening to the Street _____

Specific Needs for Now: _____

Dreams for the Future: _____

REFERENCES

AAF (American Architectural Foundation) and KnowledgeWorks Foundation. 2005. *Report from the National Summit on School Design: A Resource for Educators and Designers*. Washington, DC: KnowledgeWorks Foundation.

Ackermann, Edith K. 2004. "Constructing Knowledge and Transforming the World." In *A Learning Zone Of One's Own: Sharing Representations and Flow in Collaborative Learning Environments,* edited by Mario Tokoro and Luc Steels, 15–37. Washington, DC: IOS Press.

Alexander, Christopher, Sara Ishikawa, and Murray Silverstein. 1977. *A Pattern Language: Towns, Buildings, Construction*. New York: Oxford University Press.

Berner, Maureen M. 1993. "Building Conditions, Parental Involvement, and Student Achievement in the District of Columbia Public School System." *Urban Education* 28 (1): 6–29.

Branham, David. 2004. "The Wise Man Builds His House upon the Rock: The Effects of Inadequate School Building Infrastructure on Student Attendance." *Social Science Quarterly* 85 (5): 1112–28.

Burke, Catherine, and Ian Grosvenor. 2003. *The School I'd Like: Children and Young People's Reflections on an Education for the 21st Century*. New York: RoutledgeFalmer.

Cash, Carol Scott. 1993. "Building Condition and Student Achievement and Behavior." PhD diss. Virginia Polytechnic Institute and State University.

Clark, Alison. 2010. *Transforming Children's Spaces: Children's and Adults' Participation in Designing Learning Environments*. New York: Routledge.

Clark, Alison, and Peter Moss. 2001. *Listening to Young Children: The Mosaic Approach*. London: National Children's Bureau.

———. 2005. *Spaces to Play: More Listening to Young Children Using the Mosaic Approach*. London: National Children's Bureau.

Earthman, Glen I. 2002. "School Facility Conditions and Student Academic Achievement." UCLA: UCLA's Institute for Democracy, Education, and Access. http://escholarship.org/uc/item/5sw56439.

Earthman, Glen I., and Linda Lemasters. 1996. "Review of Research on the Relationship between School Buildings, Student Achievement, and Student Behavior." Paper presented at the annual meeting of the Council of Educational Facility Planners International, Tarpon Springs, FL, October.

Edwards, Carolyn Pope. 2002. "Three Approaches from Europe: Waldorf, Montessori, and Reggio Emilia." *Early Childhood Research and Practice* 4 (1): 1–24.

EPA (Environmental Protection Agency). 2014. "Basic Information." IAQ Design Tools for Schools. Accessed June 16. www.epa.gov/iaq/schooldesign /introduction.html.

Gaines, Kristi S., and Zane D. Curry. 2011. "The Inclusive Classroom: The Effects of Color on Learning and Behavior." *Journal of Family and Consumer Sciences Education* 29 (1): 46–57.

Ginthner, Delores. 2004. "Lighting: Its Effect on People and Spaces." *Implications* 2 (2).

Grabinger, R. Scott, and Joanna C. Dunlap. 1995. "Rich Environments for Active Learning: A Definition." *Association for Learning Technology* 3 (2): 5–34.

Halpin, David. 2007. "Utopian Spaces of 'Robust Hope': The Architecture and Nature of Progressive Learning Environments." *Asia-Pacific Journal of Teacher Education* 35 (3): 243–55.

Hines, Eric Wayne. 1996. "Building Condition and Student Achievement and Behavior." PhD diss. Virginia Polytechnic Institute and State University.

Horne Martin, Sandra. 2002. "The Classroom Environment and Its Effects on the Practice of Teachers." *Journal of Environmental Psychology* 22 (March): 139–56.

Korpela, Kalevi. 2002. "Children's Environment." In *Handbook of Environmental Psychology,* edited by Robert B. Bechtel and Arza Churchman, 363–73. New York: John Wiley & Sons.

Lackney, Jeffrey A., and Paul J. Jacobs. 2002. "Teachers as Placemakers: Investigating Teachers' Use of the Physical Environment in Instructional Design." U.S. Department of Education, Educational Resources Information Centre (ERIC) ED463645. Accessed April 28, 2014. http://files .eric.ed.gov/fulltext/ED463645.pdf.

McNamara, David R., and David G. Waugh. 1993. "Classroom Organization: A Discussion of Grouping Strategies in the Light of the 'Three Wise Men's' Report." *School Organization* 13 (1): 41–50.

Montgomery, Tim. 2008. "Space Matters: Experiences of Managing Static Formal Learning Spaces." *Active Learning in Higher Education* 9 (2): 122–38.

Nair, Prakash, Randall Fielding, and Jeffery Lackney. 2009. *The Language of School Design: Design Patterns for 21st Century Schools.* Minneapolis, MN: DesignShare.com.

Pearlman, Bob. 2010. "Designing New Learning Environments to Support 21st Century Skills." In *21st Century Skills: Rethinking How Students Learn,* edited by James A. Bellanca and Ron Brandt, 33–49. Bloomington, IN: Solution Tree Press.

Rinaldi, Carla. 1998. "The Space of Childhood." In *Children, Spaces, Relations: Metaproject for an Environment for Young Children,* edited by Giulio Ceppi and Michele Zini, 114–20. Reggio Emilia, Italy: Reggio Children.

Rivlin, Leanne G., and Carol S. Weinstein. 1984. "Educational Issues, School Settings, and Environmental Psychology." *Journal of Environmental Psychology* 4 (4): 347–64.

Strong-Wilson, Teresa, and Julia Ellis. 2007. "Children and Place: Reggio Emilia's Environment as Third Teacher." *Theory into Practice* 46 (1): 40–47.

Uhrmacher, Bruce. 2004. "An Environment of Developing Souls: The Ideas of Rudolf Steiner." In *Pedagogy of Place: Seeing Space as Cultural Education*, edited by David M. Callejo Perez, Stephen M. Fain, and Judith J. Slater, 97–120. New York: Peter Lang Publishing.

Uline, Cynthia L., Megan Tschannen-Moran, and Thomas DeVere Wolsey. 2009. "The Walls Still Speak: The Stories Occupants Tell." *Journal of Educational Administration* 47 (3): 400–426.

U.S. Department of Education. 2000. *Condition of America's Public School Facilities: 1999 (NCES 2000-032)*. Washington, DC: National Center for Education Statistics.

Woolner, Pamela, Sheila McCarter, Kate Wall, and Steve Higgins. 2012. "Changed Learning through Changed Space: When Can a Participatory Approach to the Learning Environment Challenge Preconceptions and Alter Practice?" *Improving Schools* 15 (1): 45–60.

INDEX

A

achievement
    effect of color on, 16–17
    school environment and, 16–17
acoustics, building age and, 16
adventure playgrounds, 72, 73
aesthetics of classroom design, 5–6
air-conditioning, building age and, 16
Alexander, Christopher, 21
architectural patterns and design
    aesthetic considerations, 5–6
    barriers to change, 17–18
    determining needs and dreams, 83–85
    emerging trends, 18–20
    importance of, 14–17
    involving children in, 19–20, 85
    purposes of, 21, 80
    self-study and analysis, 81–83, 86–87
    taking action for change, 85–87
    teaching philosophy, reflecting, 4, 9–14, 15
    worksheet, 89–90
attendance, school environment and, 16
attention, effect of color on, 16–17

B

behavior, effect of color on, 16–17
behavior management, classroom design and, 5
Branham, David, 16
building edges, 34, 35
bulletin boards, 38, 56

C

chairs
    child-sized, 58
    types of, 68
    See also seating arrangements
child caves, 62, 63
children
    architecture for, 14–17
    hours spent in schools, 14
    involving in school design, 19–20, 85
circulation of traffic. *See* traffic flow
Clark, Alison, 19–20
classrooms
    aesthetic considerations, 5–6
    common areas, 54, 55
    determining needs and dreams, 83–85
    evaluating, 1–3, 81–83, 86–87
    importance of design, 3–6
    outdoor spaces, 76, 77
    personal images in, 30, 31

planning and making changes to, 85–87

as relationship-oriented systems, 15–16

space differentiation in, 58, 59, 62, 63

stories told by, 84

teaching philosophy, reflecting, 4, 9–14, 15

technology considerations, 19

traffic flow, 42, 43, 59

work areas and learning zones, 28, 29, 58, 59

See also environment; school buildings

coat storage, 40, 56, 57

collaborative school design, 19–20

color schemes

    effect on learning and behavior, 16–17

    importance of, 46

    warm versus cool colors, 52, 53

common areas, 54, 55

communal eating spaces, 26, 27

community stakeholders, 86

connectivity, encouraging

    communal eating, 26, 27

    cultural diversity, 22, 23

    importance of, 22

    intimacy gradient, 24, 25, 67

    with natural world, 32, 33

    through personal documentation and images, 30, 31

    in work areas and learning zones, 28, 29

constructivist educational approach, 4, 9–10

container gardens, 75

corridors and passages

    as common areas, 54

    as usable space, 44, 45

creativity, enhancing, 28, 29

cross-curricular opportunities, gardens and, 75

cultural diversity, reflecting, 22, 23

Curry, Zane D., 16–17

D

data collection

    Mosaic approach, 20

    self-study, 82–83

design. *See* architectural patterns and design

development, effect of environment on, 14, 15–16

developmentally appropriate practices, 4–5

documentation

    self-study data collection, 82–83, 89–90

    using personal images and items, 10, 11, 30, 31

doors

    to outdoor spaces, 78, 79

    transition from street, 36, 37

dreams and needs, determining, 83–85

dropout rates, school environment and, 16

E

eating spaces, communal, 26, 27

educators. *See* staff/teachers

emotional growth and well-being, environment and, 15–16

entry zones

    building edges, 34, 35

    entrance rooms, 40, 41

    reception areas, 38, 39

    transition from street, 36, 37

environment

    aesthetic considerations, 5–6

    barriers to change, 17–18

    growth and development, effect on, 14, 15–16

    importance of, 9–15

    natural world, connectivity to, 32, 33

    as reflection of teaching philosophy, 4, 9–14, 15

    relationships, influence on, 15

    school buildings, 14–15

    technology considerations, 18–19

as "third teacher," 10

See also classrooms

Environmental Protection Agency (EPA), on school buildings, 14

exits. *See* transition spaces

F

feasibility continuum for change, 85

floor plans, drawing, 83

fluorescent lighting, 48

furniture

    chairs and sofas, 60, 61, 68, 69

    child-sized, 58

    in corridors and passages, 44, 45

    grouping children based on, 18, 58, 59

    influence on learning, 17–18

    movable, 59

    offering variety in, 68, 69

    See also seating arrangements

G

Gaines, Kristi S., 16–17

gardens, 74, 75

gazebos, 76

groups/grouping

    common areas, 54, 55

    communal eating spaces, 26, 27

    intimacy gradient, 24, 25, 67

    seating arrangements for, 18, 67

    student-centered teaching and, 17, 19

    in work areas and learning zones, 58, 59

growth and development, environment and, 14, 15–16

H

hallways. *See* corridors and passages

Halpin, David, 14

heating, building age and, 16

Houston Independent School District, 16

I

imagination. *See* creativity, enhancing

intimacy gradient, 24, 25, 67

J

Jacobs, Paul J., 18

L

Lackney, Jeffrey A., 18

lamps, 48, 49, 51

learning centers. *See* work areas and learning zones

learning styles, classroom design and, 5

lighting

    building age and, 16

    in corridors and passages, 44

    importance of, 46

    natural light, 46, 47, 52

    pools of light, creating, 48, 49

    tapestry of light and dark, 50, 51

    window places, 60, 61

light tables, 48, 51

loft areas, 62, 63, 66

M

mailboxes, 56

Martin, Sandra Horne, 17

materials
    analysis of, 83
    reflecting diversity in, 22
    "self-correcting" materials, 13
    storage spaces, 64, 65
McNamara, David R., 18
meals, communal eating, 26, 27
Montessori, Maria, 13, 29
Montessori educational approach, 4, 13–14, 29
Mosaic approach to planning and design, 19–20
Moss, Peter, 19–20
mudrooms, 56, 57

N
natural lighting
    importance of, 46, 47, 52
    window places, 60, 61
nature, incorporating into classrooms
    importance of, 33
    natural materials, 32, 33
    Waldorf approach, 4, 12
needs and dreams, determining, 83–85

O
outdoor spaces
    adventure playgrounds, 72, 73
    classroom areas, 76, 77
    gardens, 74, 75
    importance of, 72
    openings/doorways to, 78, 79
    seating, 67
    storage, 64
overhead lighting, 48

P
parents, involving, 86
passages and corridors, 44, 45
A Pattern Language: Towns, Buildings, Construction
    (Alexander, Ishikawa, and Silverstein), 21
personal spaces, 56, 57. *See also* privacy
personal stories, using images in classrooms, 30, 31
photography, as classroom analysis tool, 83
playgrounds, 72, 73
privacy
    child caves, 62, 63
    degrees of, 25
    personal spaces, 56, 57

R
reception areas, 38, 39
reframing space and design, 82
Reggio Emilia educational approach, 10, 11, 30, 31
relationship-oriented systems
    classrooms as, 10–11, 15
    common areas, 54, 55
    communal eating spaces, 26, 27
    intimacy gradients, 24, 25
    meaningful images, displaying, 10, 11, 30, 31
Rivlin, Leanne G., 14
room structure
    analysis of, 81–83
    child caves, 62, 63
    common areas at the heart, 54, 55
    personal spaces, 56, 57
    space differentiation, 58, 59, 62, 63
    storage areas, 64, 65
    window places, 60, 61, 71
    See also classrooms

S

safety apparel, 29
school buildings
    achievement, influence on, 16–17
    collaborative/participatory design of, 19–20. 85–86
    condition and age of, 14–15, 16
    funding needs, 14–15
    growth and development, influence on, 14, 15–16
    hours spent in, 14
    traditional seating arrangements, 17–18
    See also classrooms
seating arrangements
    chairs and sofas, 60, 61, 68, 69
    effect on learning, 17–18
    entrance zones, 38, 39, 40, 41
    grouping children, 18, 58, 59
    intimacy gradient, 24, 25, 67
    offering variety in, 66, 67
    outdoors, 67
    stair seats, 70, 71
    window places, 60, 61, 71
    in work areas and learning zones, 17, 19, 58, 59
    See also furniture
self-study tool kit, 81–83, 89–90
shoe storage, 40, 56, 57
sofas, 61, 69
space management
    analysis of, 81–83
    corridors and passages, 44, 45
    traffic flow, 42, 43, 59
    See also architectural patterns and design;
        room structure

staff/teachers
    common areas for, 55
    involving in design, 82–83, 85
    personal spaces for, 56
    teacher preparation programs, 18
stairways
    stair seats, 70, 71
    as usable space, 44
stakeholders
    involving in school design, 19–20, 85–86
    recruiting assistance from, 82–83
Steiner, Rudolf, 12
storage
    bulk materials, 64, 65
    outdoor structures, 64
    personal items, 56, 57
stories, defining for classrooms, 84
student-centered teaching methods, 17–18, 19
sunlight. *See* natural lighting
supplies, storage of, 64, 65

T

task distribution chart, developing, 85–86
teacher-directed teaching methods, 17–18, 19
teacher preparation programs, 18
teachers. *See* staff/teachers
teaching philosophy
    reflecting in classroom design, 4, 9–14, 15
    stories told by classrooms, 84
technology, learning environments and, 18–19
timeline for change, developing, 86
tool kits
    classroom analysis and self-study, 81–83
    generating ideas, 83–85
    taking action for change, 85–87
    worksheet, 89–90

traffic flow
    corridors and passages, 44, 45
    importance of managing, 42, 59
    between and within rooms, 42, 43
transition spaces
    building edges, 34, 35
    entrance rooms, 40, 41
    importance of, 34
    reception areas, 38, 39
    from street to door, 36, 37
trees, as child caves, 62

U

U.S. Environmental Protection Agency (EPA),
    on school buildings, 14

V

ventilation, building age and, 16
visual displays, of personal images, 10, 11, 30, 31

W

Waldorf educational approach, 4, 12
Waugh, David G., 18
Weinstein, Carol S., 14
window places, 60, 61, 71
work areas and learning zones
    analysis of, 83
    creating, 28, 29
    group arrangements, 18, 58, 59
    Montessori approach, 4, 13–14, 29
    traffic flow between, 42, 43, 59